D1537032

Follow the Directions!

Grades 1–3

by Denise Nessel, Ph.D. and Joyce Marie Graham, Ph.D.

SCHOLASTIC
PROFESSIONAL BOOKS

NEW YORK • TORONTO • LONDON • AUCKLAND • SYDNEY
MEXICO CITY • NEW DELHI • HONG KONG • BUENOS AIRES

To Ford, whose support and help with this project, as with so much else, is appreciated more than he knows. —D.N.

To my mother, Esther Graham Ciccioli, who instilled in me the love of learning. —J.M.G

Scholastic Inc. grants teachers permission to photocopy the reproducible pages from this book for classroom use. No other part of this publication may be reproduced in whole or in part, or stored in a retrieval system, or transmitted in any form or by any means, electronic, mechanical, photocopying, recording, or otherwise, without written permission of the publisher. For information regarding permission, write to Scholastic Inc., 555 Broadway, New York, NY 10012.

Cover design by Norma Ortiz
Interior design by Solutions by Design, Inc.
Interior illustrations by Maxie Chambliss

ISBN: 0-439-21861-6

Copyright © 2001 by Denise Nessel and Joyce Marie Graham
All rights reserved. Printed in the U.S.A.

CONTENTS

Introduction

In the early grades, children learn many skills that affect their success throughout their school lives. One of the most important is the skill of understanding and following directions, both oral and written. The sooner children learn to handle directions of all kinds, the more effective they become because they can proceed on their own without needing the teacher to lead them step by step. Such independence becomes more and more important as they move through the grades and encounter more sophisticated learning activities, tests they must complete entirely on their own, and teachers who expect greater levels of independence. If very young students become dependent on their teachers to lead them through every task, the demands for independence in later grades can be perplexing and frustrating.

There isn't one surefire solution to this widespread problem, but the activities in this book offer an approach that works. These easy-to-read, step-by-step exercises give children essential practice following both oral and written directions while reinforcing primary skills such as reading, counting, classifying, and more. Learning to follow directions helps children become independent and effective learners, which boosts their performance in class and on tests.

From Dependence to Independence

Children very quickly develop habits of dependence on the teacher. In the first week of kindergarten, they learn that following directions is very important. They soon learn to wait for the teacher to tell them what to do, whether they're lining up to leave the classroom, working on a lesson, or starting a project. Of course, these habits are very useful. Children will work more effectively and productively when the teacher has given them direction and purpose. On the other hand, when children can't figure some things out on their own, their productivity and sense of accomplishment suffer. Think of the children who line up at the teacher's desk with papers in hand to ask what to do next, or the children who sit at their desks with their hands in the air, waiting for the teacher to help them.

Balance is the key. Even the youngest children need to know both how to follow the teacher's directions and how to proceed on their own. In the primary grades, children are led much more often than they are encouraged to function independently, and this imbalance may lead to overdependence on the teacher. To bring things into balance, primary-grade children need many more opportunities to figure things out on their own. At first, when they realize the teacher isn't going to help them, they may become anxious or frustrated. As they become more independent, they enjoy their increasing competence.

The approach to achieving balance is straightforward: Each day, present a new, short set of directions for children to follow independently. We've created 180 sets of directions on reproducible cards for you to use with your students—one for each day of the school year. Since many children at these grade levels are just beginning to read, these directions are simple and include highly familiar words. The directions are quick and easy for children to complete, so the focus is on the directions, not on how to do the activity.

These directions are different from those given for work in regular subjects, such as math or reading. They're used only to help children gain competence in following directions. But as children improve their ability with these special tasks, they can transfer their skills to a variety of directions that they will encounter in their regular subjects.

How to Use This Book

The 180 sets of directions in this book are conveniently organized into nine sections of similar tasks so that you can begin with the kind of activities that are most suitable for your class. If your students have had little experience with following written directions independently, you'll probably want to start with the easiest tasks at the beginning of the book and work up to the more challenging activities.

The first section of directions uses a small set of words in different combinations. The limited number of words allows children to focus on the directions rather than on trying to recognize and read the words. Each section of directions builds on earlier sets, using previously learned words along with a few new words for that group. By seeing the same words frequently and in different sentences, children will master the words while also getting meaningful practice with directions. (If your students don't already know the words in a section, refer to Teaching New Vocabulary Words on pages 8–10. On pages 64–80, you'll find reproducible word cards to help teach the words in Sections 1–5 and 7.)

The directions involve simple tasks that are related to typical primary-grade skill objectives, so they can help your students develop those skills. Examples include coloring or drawing simple images, writing letters or numbers, and cutting things out and pasting them onto construction paper in a specified order or location. Many of the tasks involve using reproducible activity sheets that accompany the directions, making the program very easy to use.

The activities in this book can be used to give children practice with both written and oral directions. The directions in Section 6 are designed to be presented orally, but reproducible cards are also provided in case you choose to present them as written directions. You might decide to present any of the other sections orally as well. To give children practice seeing the same directions in writing after first hearing them, present a set of directions orally, and then give children the same set of directions on the reproducible card.

The activities are designed to be flexible and easy to use. You can use them all just as they're presented here, or you can select the ones that are most suited to your own objectives. Feel free to use this book as a starting point for developing your own activities or even your own creative program for teaching the skill of following directions.

How to Be Successful With These Activities

Teachers are most successful with these activities when they give one set of directions every day rather than using only a few from time to time. Regular, frequent practice is best for helping children develop solid skills and habits of independence. This is especially important at the beginning. Once your students are comfortable following directions on their own, you may want to change the routines a bit, as suggested in The Ongoing Effort section on page 12. Here are some other tips to get started:

Set short- and long-term goals.

Tell students that you want everyone in the class to be able to follow directions independently. Discuss what the word *independent* means and ask them to think of things that they can do independently. Explain that you would like students to be able to follow directions without your having to explain anything, including that there are directions to be followed. Tell students that this is a long-term goal and that you'll help them work up to it with a series of easy-to-reach, short-term goals.

Explain the importance of independence.

Discuss with children the value of both waiting to be told what to do and figuring things out independently. Tell students you want them to wait for your guidance some of the time and to figure things out on their own at other times. Point out that when they do figure some things out on their own, they'll be that much more competent with their schoolwork and with the things they do outside of school.

Give recognition for effort as well as correct responses.

The purpose of this program is to encourage children to figure things out on their own, so it's a good idea to commend their efforts even when their responses aren't accurate. The child who makes small errors but who puts effort into figuring out what to do will become more accurate with time. Express enthusiasm for the students' efforts, and encourage children to share their work and praise one another for their accomplishments.

Establish routines.

In the beginning, it is especially helpful to children if you follow a predictable routine. For instance, clear a space on the chalkboard or set up an easel with chart paper, and put the directions in that spot every day. This will help focus children's attention on the directions. You may also want to set up a special Directions Basket where children can turn in their finished work. These routines will reduce confusion and wasted time when students are working on these activities.

Invite reflection and self-evaluation.

At first, take time after each activity to have a few students tell what they did well and what they found difficult. Commend them for their reflective thinking and encourage them to share ideas that will help everyone be more successful at following the directions in these activities. Just a few minutes a day of talking about how they're doing will help students become more aware of their work and more attentive when they try the next activity. Here are some questions that can help young children reflect on the tasks and their approaches to them:

❀ How do you think you did today with the directions activity? Thumbs up if you did very well; thumbs down if you could have done a better job.

❀ What was the easiest part? The hardest?

❀ Will you do anything differently when you have another activity like this one?

❀ How can you be sure you have followed directions correctly?

Make it fun!

Treat this program more as an ongoing game than high-stakes academic work. Students are more likely to respond positively if they see the activities as amusing and interesting rather than as a difficult task at which they might fail. To keep the tone light and positive, make colorful posters or banners about following directions and post them in the room along with a few balloons, streamers, or other festive decorations.

Teaching New Vocabulary Words

If your students are just learning to read, start by teaching the vocabulary words that appear in Section 1 before asking children to complete these activities. A list of the new vocabulary words that appear in each of the first seven sections is provided in the Section-by-Section Guide on pages 13–22. Reproducible word cards are also provided for those words on pages 64–80. (Section 6 is designed to

be presented orally and Sections 8 and 9 are designed for more proficient readers.)

Here are some suggestions for introducing and teaching new vocabulary words. The steps below describe one method of teaching the words from Section 1. The same procedures can be followed to teach new vocabulary words in subsequent sections as well. Because each section incorporates words from the previous sections, children will have a lot of exposure to these words and probably will not need you to reteach them for each section.

Day 1

In advance, review the word list for Section 1 and then read through the direction cards for Section 1 on pages 24–25. Start by teaching children the four color words (*red, blue, green,* and *yellow*). Write the words on the chalkboard or on chart paper, or photocopy and display the word cards on pages 65–66. Point to the word *red* while you say it. Then have children say it with you several times. Tape a small piece of red paper beside the word so children will associate the word with the color it stands for. Say the word together. Do the same with the other three words. Then review each word again. Remove the pieces of colored paper from the board. Invite children to take turns matching the pieces of colored paper to the right words, saying the words each time. Do this matching activity several times until children are familiar with the meanings of the four words.

Day 2

Review the color words again by having children repeat the above matching activity two or three times. Then write the four object words on the board (*dog, flower, house,* and *car*) and have pictures of the objects available to tape beside the words. (Use the pictures from Activity Sheet A on page 57 for this purpose, or use your own pictures of these objects.) Follow the same procedure for teaching these words that you followed for the color words. Review all eight words at the end of the lesson. For additional reinforcement, invite children to review these eight words independently. In a learning center, provide the word cards for the words, the pieces of colored paper, and the pictures. Children can work in pairs or small groups to match the word cards with either the appropriate picture or colored paper.

Day 3

Review the color and object words, using the colored paper and pictures for two or three rounds of the matching activity. Then write the three verbs on the board (*circle, underline,* and *color*). Draw a circle beside *circle,* draw a line under *underline,* and color an area next to *color.* Explain each action to help children associate the word with its meaning. Point to one of the words and have a child come to the board and complete the correct action (circling, underlining, or coloring). Write the word *the* on the board and have children say it with you

several times. Create several simple sentences such as: "Color the dog red," or "Underline the flower." Have children read the sentences and complete the specified action.

Day 4

You'll need four markers (red, blue, green, and yellow) and chart paper. Review all of the words from the previous three days and then introduce the remaining words (*follow, directions, it, write, your, name*). On chart paper, draw a large flower. Above the flower, write the following:

> **Follow the Directions:**
>
> **Color the flower red.**
>
> **Underline it.**

Have children read the words silently and raise their hands when they understand what to do. When many hands have been raised, invite a volunteer to read the directions aloud and then complete the activity. Present two or three similar directions, changing key words each time. Ask a different student to read and then follow the directions each time.

Guided Practice With Activity Sheets

Once children have learned the new vocabulary words, they will need some guided practice with the first Activity Sheet to get started. Here's a suggested sequence:

1. On chart paper, draw a simple house. Write the following above the house:

   > **Follow the Directions:**
   >
   > **Circle the house.**
   >
   > **Color it blue.**

2. Ask children to read the directions silently and raise their hands when they know what the words say. When many hands have been raised, call on one child to read the directions aloud, come up to the chart paper, and follow the directions. If children need additional guided practice, give them a few other similar sets of directions to read and follow, using the same procedures as above.

3. Give each child a copy of Activity Sheet A. On the board or chart paper, write the directions from the first card of Section 1. Have children read the directions silently and then follow the directions, using crayons or markers on their activity sheet. Walk around the room, observing children's progress. When everyone has finished, have children share their work with their neighbors and talk about what they did. Then tell the class that they will have a similar set of directions to follow the next day and that you want them to try to follow those directions on their own without relying on you to explain anything.

4. Decide on a place in the room for posting the directions each day. You could print them on a clear space on the board or on a flip chart displayed on an easel. Or you might use a pocket chart, arranging the reproducible word cards each day in the appropriate order. If you would like children to read their own set of directions, photocopy the reproducible direction cards, cut along the dashed lines, and distribute.

5. The next day, give each child another copy of Activity Sheet A. Post the directions from the second card in Section 1. Call children's attention to the directions, saying something like this:

> *I'm sure you remember the directions we followed together yesterday. Here's another set. This time, I want you to follow them on your own. Read the directions and think about what they say. Then do the work on your activity sheet.*

Let children figure out the directions by themselves. If someone says, "What are we supposed to do?" simply reply, "Read the directions and follow them. I know you can figure them out on your own." Once you say this, it's very important to stick with it. Provide encouragement, but don't provide help. If students seem frustrated, simply tell them to do their best and remind them that the purpose of the activity is for them to figure out the directions on their own.

If many students have difficulty with this first independent attempt, provide more guided practice that day or try again the next day. If children are very dependent on your help, it may take them several days to feel comfortable following the directions on their own. However, the sooner they learn to do this, the sooner they'll benefit. If children are having difficulty reading the words, try following the steps for teaching new vocabulary on pages 8–10. Or, present the directions orally until children's reading skills are stronger.

At the end of children's first independent attempt, tell them that you will post a new set of directions in the same place the next day and that you expect them to look for the directions and follow them without any reminders or guidance from you. Set a time for the directions activity, such as first thing in the morning or right after lunch.

6. Post a new set of directions each day so that children will get into a routine of looking for the directions and following them at the set time. Students often remind each other to complete the task each day. We think reminders should be allowed because, in the world outside of school, people regularly remind each other of important things they need to do. In other words, we don't consider this "cheating" because it's a natural response. We suggest you allow this while also encouraging students to be more and more responsible for themselves.

The Ongoing Effort

When you're ready to start each section, read through the direction cards to decide which ones you want to use and which ones you want to modify or replace. We encourage you to adapt the activities and add your own to best meet your students' needs.

Because of time constraints and schedule changes, you may not be able to give your students a set of directions every day. Try to keep to the routine as often as possible so that students will get into the habit of looking for directions to follow at the set time. These tasks can be great warm-up activities, or you may find they're useful for settling children down after lunch. Experiment with different times of day to see what works best for your class.

After the first month or two, you may want to vary the routine a bit to keep interest high. For instance, you could present a set of directions every day for two weeks, take a week off, present a set of directions every day for another two weeks, and so on. Or, present a set of directions only on Mondays, Wednesdays, and Fridays. Alternatively, have children complete a directions activity each day, Monday through Thursday, with no activity on Friday.

Assessment

At first, you'll probably want to check children's work yourself to see how they are doing. You may want to collect the papers and check them at a later time, or you may want to circulate around the room and check students' work as they are completing the task. You might also have pairs of students exchange papers and check each other's work.

You may wish to make these for-credit activities, giving children a grade for successful completion of a task. On the other hand, the daily practice alone is all that's needed for most children to increase their abilities, so grading isn't really necessary.

We hope you'll find this book a good resource for helping your students develop a useful skill while having fun with some interesting tasks!

Section-by-Section Guide

Section 1

This section includes 12 sets of directions. Each set appears on its own reproducible card on pages 24–25. Each child needs a copy of Activity Sheet A on page 57 to complete each set of directions.

To Do

✿ Teach the key words for this section if children don't already know them. (See pages 8–10 for a suggested teaching method. Reproducible word cards for this instruction appear on pages 64–80.)

✿ Read the direction cards and decide which ones you want to use.

✿ Make copies of Activity Sheet A.

✿ Make copies of the direction cards on pages 24–25 (optional).

✿ Set up a directions area in the room. You might write the directions on the board or chart paper, or designate a spot where children can find copies of the direction cards. Store copies of the activity sheets and any necessary supplies in the same area.

✿ Establish a routine for collecting papers. You may want to collect them yourself, ask a volunteer to collect them, or have children put them in a special directions basket.

New Words

follow	dog
directions	flower
circle	house
underline	car
color	it
red	the
blue	write
green	your
yellow	name

Section 2

This section includes 18 sets of directions. The words from Section 1 are used in these directions, along with eight new words. The directions are very similar to those in Section 1, but include additional words for colors and objects. Each child needs a copy of Activity Sheet B on page 58 to complete each set of directions.

To Do

✿ Teach the new words for this section if children don't already know them.

✿ Read the direction cards and decide which ones you want to use.

✿ Make copies of Activity Sheet B.

✿ Make copies of the direction cards on pages 26–28 (optional).

✿ Follow your established procedures for posting directions and collecting papers.

New Words

brown
black
purple
orange
cat
tree
book
sun

Section 3

This section includes 24 sets of directions. The words from Sections 1 and 2 are used in these directions, along with five new words and one word (*circle*) that is used as a noun instead of a verb. The directions are similar to those in Sections 1 and 2, but include additional words for objects and actions. Also, the heading is simply the word "Directions" instead of "Follow the Directions." Each child needs a copy of Activity Sheet C on page 59 to complete each set of directions.

To Do

✿ Teach the new words for this section if children don't already know them.

✿ Read the direction cards and decide which ones you want to use.

✿ Make copies of Activity Sheet C.

✿ Make copies of the direction cards on pages 29–32 (optional).

✿ Follow your established procedures for posting directions and collecting papers.

New Words

circle
(used as a noun
instead of a verb)

square

triangle

rectangle

cross

out

Section 4

This section includes 24 sets of directions. Words from previous sections are used in these directions, along with six new words. The directions are similar to those presented so far, but some additional words for actions are included. Also, two activity sheets are needed for each activity: Activity Sheet C on page 59 and Activity Sheet D on page 60. Each child needs a copy of both sheets to complete each set of directions.

To Do

✿ Teach the new words for this section if children don't already know them.

✿ Read the direction cards and decide which ones you want to use.

✿ Make copies of Activity Sheet C and Activity Sheet D.

✿ Make copies of the direction cards on pages 33–36 (optional).

✿ Follow your established procedures for posting directions and collecting papers.

New Words

paste
onto
cut
over
under
inside

Section 5

This section includes 18 sets of directions. Words from previous sections are used in these directions, along with nine new words. The directions are similar to those presented so far, but children complete these activities on their own paper. An activity sheet is not needed. The directions in this section are a bit more complicated, offering a greater challenge and increasing children's interest.

To Do

✿ Teach the new words for this section if children don't already know them.

✿ Read the direction cards and decide which ones you want to use.

✿ Make copies of the direction cards on pages 37–39 (optional).

✿ Provide children with a choice of colored paper: white, red, yellow, and blue. Explain to children that if the directions do not specify a color of paper, they may choose any color.

✿ Follow your established procedures for posting directions and collecting papers.

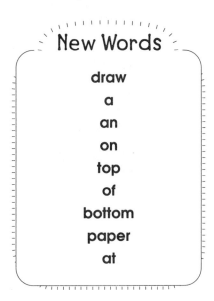

New Words

draw
a
an
on
top
of
bottom
paper
at

Section 6

This section includes 24 sets of directions. These directions are different in that they are designed to be presented orally, rather than in writing. Words from previous sections are used in these directions, along with a number of new words. The new words are not introduced (and are not provided on reproducible word cards) because children are almost certain to be familiar with them from hearing them frequently both inside and outside of school. (If you would like to present the directions in this section as a written exercise, reproducible direction cards are provided on pages 40–43.)

Each child needs a copy of Activity Sheet E on page 61 to complete each set of directions. This activity sheet is different in that it has more images, allowing greater variety and complexity in the activities. Because these directions are more complicated than the ones in earlier groups, they provide a greater challenge and increase children's interest.

We suggest that at first you read aloud a direction two or three times to make sure students have processed what to do. But after a few days of this, we suggest you introduce a goal of reading aloud the daily direction only once. Children will need practice adapting to this new routine. Because children are used to having adults repeat things, they often don't listen carefully. But if you tell them you will not repeat and stick to that rule, they will soon learn to listen carefully and grasp the information the first time around.

To Do

✿ Read the direction cards and decide which ones you want to use.

✿ Make copies of Activity Sheet E.

✿ Explain the change in procedure from written to oral directions and encourage children to listen carefully as you read a set of directions each day.

✿ Follow your established procedures for collecting papers.

Section 7

This section includes 24 sets of directions. The directions are based on those in Section 6, which were presented orally. These directions are intended to be presented in writing. Each child needs a copy of Activity Sheet E on page 61 to complete each set of directions.

Many of the object words from this section and previous sections appear in the plural form (*bears, birds, cats, circles, flowers, rabbits, squares,* and *trees*). The action words from previous sections are sometimes used in the past tense (*colored* and *crossed*). This is a good opportunity to teach children how to form both plural nouns and verbs in the past tense. In addition, 20 new words are introduced. Children are likely to know most of the words already from seeing them in print. Although the new words are listed below, we suggest you teach only the ones that you think children do not know.

To Do

❀ Teach the key words for this set if children don't already know them.

❀ Read the direction cards and decide which ones you want to use.

❀ Make copies of Activity Sheet E.

❀ Make copies of the direction cards on pages 44–47 (optional).

❀ Explain the change in procedure from oral to written directions and encourage children to read carefully.

❀ Follow your established procedures for posting directions and collecting papers.

New Words

one	white
two	count
three	number
four	line
five	things
six	you
bear	and
rabbit	that
fish	them
bird	all

Section 8

This section includes 20 sets of directions. These activities are more complicated and are designed for proficient readers. The directions include a number of words that have not been introduced previously in this book. New words are not listed for this section and are not provided on reproducible word cards because children are likely to know most of the words already from seeing them in print. If you think the directions are too difficult for your students to read independently, you can present them orally instead.

In some of these activities, children are directed to put their papers in a directions basket and in others to leave their papers on their desks for you to collect. Tell children to watch for this difference at the outset, but try not to help them from day to day so that each day they must think about what they are supposed to do with their papers.

To Do

❀ Read the direction cards and decide which ones you want to use.

❀ Make copies of the direction cards on pages 48–52 (optional).

❀ Gather paper and other supplies for the activities children will complete.

❀ Follow your established procedures for posting directions and collecting papers.

Section 9

This section includes 16 sets of directions. These activities involve making simple projects that can be displayed in the classroom or taken home. Some of the projects can be made several times throughout the year, such as birthday cards.

The activities in this section are more complicated and are designed for proficient readers. The directions include a number of words that have not been introduced previously in the book. New words are not listed for this section but children are likely to know most of the words already from seeing them in print. Since these activities are designed for students who are reading well, word cards are not presented for teaching new vocabulary. If the directions in this section are too difficult for your students to read, present them orally instead.

To Do

❀ Read the direction cards and decide which ones you want to use.

❀ Make copies of the direction cards on pages 53–56 (optional).

❀ Read the preparation steps listed below for each set of directions. Make any necessary copies and gather supplies.

❀ Follow your established procedures for posting directions and collecting papers.

Preparation

Set 1. Provide white construction paper, pencils, crayons, and scissors. Cut a large circle from a sturdy sheet of paper. Cut a hole in the middle to make the shape of a wreath. Paste the hands children create onto the wreath and display the finished collaborative project in the classroom or hallway with a caption such as "We join hands in friendship."

Set 2. Put white drawing paper in the directions basket. On the chalkboard, print the heading "How We Feel Today." When children turn in their drawings, tape them to the board under the heading.

Set 3. Put white drawing paper in the directions basket. Provide pencils and tape. On the chalkboard, print the heading "Friends." When children are done, they should tape their papers onto the board.

Set 4. Put white drawing paper in the directions basket. Provide pencils and crayons or markers. After you've checked their papers, have children take them home.

Sets 5–9. Make copies of Activity Sheet F on page 62 and put them in the directions basket. Provide construction paper and crayons or markers. After you've checked their papers, encourage children to take them home.

Set 10. Provide magazines and newspapers, scissors, paste, and red construction paper. After you've checked their papers, encourage children to take them home.

Set 11. Provide magazines and newspapers, scissors, paste, and green construction paper. After you've checked their papers, encourage children to take them home.

Set 12. Draw two or three different clown faces on paper plates and post them on the board. Put plain white paper plates in the directions basket. Provide colored markers. Encourage children to take home their finished clown faces.

Set 13. Put plain white paper plates in the directions basket. Provide colored markers. Encourage children to take their finished projects home.

Set 14. On drawing paper, draw a face as a model. Post the face on the board for children to see as they work. Put plain white drawing paper in the directions basket. Provide pencils and crayons or markers. Encourage children to take home their finished drawings.

Set 15. Put lined paper in the directions basket. When children have turned in their papers, post the finished projects on the board.

Set 16. Have children do this activity when it is someone's birthday. On the directions, fill in the number of candles children should draw. Put construction paper in the directions basket. When children have turned in their cards, put them in the birthday child's cubby or make a special birthday mailbox. The birthday child can take the cards out of the mailbox, or you may appoint a "mail carrier" to retrieve the cards and deliver them to the birthday child.

Reproducible
Direction Cards

Section 1

1
Follow the Directions:

Circle the dog.

Color it red.

Write your name.

2
Follow the Directions:

Underline the flower.

Color it yellow.

Write your name.

3
Follow the Directions:

Color the house blue.

Circle it.

Write your name.

4
Follow the Directions:

Color the car green.

Underline it.

Write your name.

5
Follow the Directions:

Color the dog yellow.

Underline it.

Write your name.

6
Follow the Directions:

Color the house yellow.

Circle it.

Write your name.

Follow the Directions! Scholastic Professional Books

Section 1

7 **Follow the Directions:**	8 **Follow the Directions:**
Color the flower blue. Underline it. Write your name.	Circle the dog. Color it blue. Write your name.
9 **Follow the Directions:**	10 **Follow the Directions:**
Color the flower red. Circle it. Write your name.	Color the car red. Underline it. Write your name.
11 **Follow the Directions:**	12 **Follow the Directions:**
Color the car blue. Circle it. Write your name.	Underline the house. Color it green. Write your name.

Section 2

1
Follow the Directions:

Circle the cat.

Color it brown.

Write your name.

2
Follow the Directions:

Underline the tree.

Color it orange.

Write your name.

3
Follow the Directions:

Color the book black.

Circle it.

Write your name.

4
Follow the Directions:

Color the sun purple.

Underline it.

Write your name.

5
Follow the Directions:

Color the cat orange.

Underline it.

Write your name.

6
Follow the Directions:

Circle the book.

Color it purple.

Write your name.

Follow the Directions! Scholastic Professional Books

7

Follow the Directions:

Color the tree black.

Underline it.

Write your name.

8

Follow the Directions:

Circle the cat.

Color it black.

Write your name.

9

Follow the Directions:

Color the cat brown.

Circle it.

Write your name.

10

Follow the Directions:

Color the book brown.

Underline it.

Write your name.

11

Follow the Directions:

Circle the sun.

Color it purple.

Write your name.

12

Follow the Directions:

Color the book orange.

Circle it.

Write your name.

13

Follow the Directions:

Circle the cat.

Color it purple.

Write your name.

14

Follow the Directions:

Underline the tree.

Color it purple.

Write your name.

15

Follow the Directions:

Color the book brown.

Circle it.

Write your name.

16

Follow the Directions:

Color the sun orange.

Underline it.

Write your name.

17

Follow the Directions:

Color the sun brown.

Underline it.

Write your name.

18

Follow the Directions:

Circle the tree.

Color it brown.

Write your name.

28

Section 3

1

Directions:

Cross out the square.

Color it red.

Write your name.

2

Directions:

Underline the rectangle.

Color it yellow.

Write your name.

3

Directions:

Color the circle blue.

Cross it out.

Write your name.

4

Directions:

Color the rectangle purple.

Cross it out.

Write your name.

5

Directions:

Color the triangle green.

Underline it.

Write your name.

6

Directions:

Color the square yellow.

Underline it.

Write your name.

Section 3

7

Directions:

Color the circle orange.

Cross it out.

Write your name.

8

Directions:

Color the rectangle blue.

Underline it.

Write your name.

9

Directions:

Cross out the square.

Color it black.

Write your name.

10

Directions:

Color the rectangle red.

Cross it out.

Write your name.

11

Directions:

Color the triangle brown.

Underline it.

Write your name.

12

Directions:

Cross out the square.

Underline it.

Write your name.

Follow the Directions! Scholastic Professional Books

Section 3

13

Directions:

Cross out the circle.

Color it blue.

Write your name.

14

Directions:

Color the triangle purple.

Cross it out.

Write your name.

15

Directions:

Cross out the rectangle.

Underline it.

Write your name.

16

Directions:

Underline the circle.

Color it orange.

Write your name.

17

Directions:

Cross out the square.

Color it green.

Write your name.

18

Directions:

Cross out the circle.

Underline it.

Write your name.

Section 3

19

Directions:

Underline the rectangle.

Color it black.

Write your name.

20

Directions:

Color the circle red.

Cross it out.

Write your name.

21

Directions:

Color the triangle yellow.

Underline it.

Write your name.

22

Directions:

Cross out the triangle.

Underline it.

Write your name.

23

Directions:

Underline the triangle.

Color it red.

Write your name.

24

Directions:

Color the triangle green.

Cross it out.

Write your name.

Follow the Directions! Scholastic Professional Books

Section 4

1

Follow the Directions:

Color the cat yellow.

Cut it out.

Paste it onto the square.

Write your name.

2

Follow the Directions:

Cut out the book.

Color it brown.

Paste it onto the rectangle.

Write your name.

3

Follow the Directions:

Cut out the dog.

Color it purple.

Paste it onto the circle.

Write your name.

4

Follow the Directions:

Color the cat brown.

Cut it out.

Paste it over the triangle.

Write your name.

5

Follow the Directions:

Color the house purple.

Cut it out.

Paste it onto the square.

Write your name.

6

Follow the Directions:

Cut out the tree.

Color it brown.

Paste it inside the circle.

Write your name.

7

Follow the Directions:

Cut out the book.

Color it black.

Paste it over the triangle.

Write your name.

8

Follow the Directions:

Color the car red.

Cut it out.

Paste it onto the triangle.

Write your name.

9

Follow the Directions:

Cut out the cat.

Color it black.

Paste it inside the rectangle.

Write your name.

10

Follow the Directions:

Color the book blue.

Cut it out.

Paste it onto the circle.

Write your name.

11

Follow the Directions:

Cut out the flower.

Color it red.

Paste it under the square.

Write your name.

12

Follow the Directions:

Cut out the sun.

Color it orange.

Paste it inside the square.

Write your name.

Follow the Directions! Scholastic Professional Books

Section 4

13

Follow the Directions:

Color the car brown.

Cut it out.

Paste it over the circle.

Write your name.

14

Follow the Directions:

Color the sun red.

Cut it out.

Paste it under the rectangle.

Write your name.

15

Follow the Directions:

Color the dog black.

Cut it out.

Paste it under the square.

Write your name.

16

Follow the Directions:

Color the tree orange.

Cut it out.

Paste it onto the circle.

Write your name.

17

Follow the Directions:

Cut out the dog.

Color it blue.

Paste it onto the triangle.

Write your name.

18

Follow the Directions:

Color the tree green.

Cut it out.

Paste it over the triangle.

Write your name.

19

Follow the Directions:

Cut out the house.

Color it orange.

Paste it under the square.

Write your name.

20

Follow the Directions:

Color the sun yellow.

Cut it out.

Paste it onto the circle.

Write your name.

21

Follow the Directions:

Cut out the house.

Color it green.

Paste it onto the rectangle.

Write your name.

22

Follow the Directions:

Color the flower yellow.

Cut it out.

Paste it over the triangle.

Write your name.

23

Follow the Directions:

Cut out the flower.

Color it purple.

Paste it under the square.

Write your name.

24

Follow the Directions:

Color the car blue.

Cut it out.

Paste it inside the circle.

Write your name.

Follow the Directions! Scholastic Professional Books

Section 5

1

Follow the Directions:

Write your name on the paper.

Draw a circle under your name.

Color the circle red.

2

Follow the Directions:

Draw a flower.

Cut it out.

Paste it onto red paper.

Write your name on the paper.

3

Follow the Directions:

Write your name on the paper.

Underline it.

Draw a square under your name.

4

Follow the Directions:

Draw a tree.

Cut it out.

Paste it onto yellow paper.

Write your name on the paper.

5

Follow the Directions:

Draw a triangle.

Draw an orange flower inside the triangle.

Underline the triangle

Write your name at the top of the paper.

6

Follow the Directions:

Draw a triangle.

Color it blue.

Draw a yellow sun over the triangle.

Write your name at the bottom of the paper.

Section 5

7

Follow the Directions:

Draw a rectangle.

Draw a red dog inside the rectangle.

Underline the dog.

Write your name on the paper.

8

Follow the Directions:

Draw a black cat, a yellow flower, and a green tree.

Underline the cat.

Write your name at the top of the paper.

9

Follow the Directions:

Draw a circle.

Draw a triangle inside the circle.

Color the triangle red.

Underline the circle.

Write your name on the paper.

10

Follow the Directions:

Draw an orange sun over a red house.

Circle the house.

Write your name on the paper.

11

Follow the Directions:

Draw a square.

Color it green.

Cut it out.

Paste it onto blue paper.

Write your name at the top of the paper.

12

Follow the Directions:

Draw a square.

Write your name inside the square.

Draw an orange flower under the square.

Underline the flower.

Follow the Directions! Scholastic Professional Books

Section 5

13 Follow the Directions:

Write your name on the paper.

Underline it.

Draw a rectangle under your name.

Color the rectangle yellow.

14 Follow the Directions:

Draw a circle.

Write your name inside the circle.

Draw an orange flower under the circle.

Underline the flower.

15 Follow the Directions:

Draw a brown cat.

Draw a red house.

Draw a circle around the cat and the house.

Write your name on the paper.

16 Follow the Directions:

Draw a cat, a house, a triangle, and a flower.

Cross out the triangle.

Color the cat yellow.

Color the flower red.

Write your name on the paper.

17 Follow the Directions:

Draw a circle.

Draw a flower under the circle.

Color the flower red.

Color the circle yellow.

Write your name on the paper.

18 Follow the Directions:

Write your name inside a circle.

Draw a red flower inside a square.

Underline your name.

Underline the red flower.

1

Follow the Directions:

Color four circles blue.

Write your name at the bottom of the paper.

2

Follow the Directions:

Color two bears red.

Color two rabbits yellow.

Write your name at the top of the paper.

3

Follow the Directions:

Color three flowers blue.

Color two squares red.

Count the number of things you colored and circle that number.

Write your name at the bottom of the paper.

4

Follow the Directions:

Cross out three fish and three birds.

Count the number of things you crossed out and circle that number.

Write your name at the top of the paper.

5

Follow the Directions:

Cut out three bears.

Paste them onto red paper.

Write your name on the red paper.

6

Follow the Directions:

Cut out two rabbits and one flower.

Paste them onto a sheet of yellow paper.

Write your name on the yellow paper.

Follow the Directions! Scholastic Professional Books

Section 6

7

Follow the Directions:

Color three fish blue, four cats orange, and one rabbit yellow.

Circle two trees.

Write your name at the top of the paper.

8

Follow the Directions:

Circle the number five.

Color all the squares red.

Write your name at the bottom of the paper.

9

Follow the Directions:

Color four squares blue.

Color three cats yellow.

Count the number of things you colored and circle that number.

Write your name at the bottom of the paper.

10

Follow the Directions:

Color all the cats red.

Color all the fish blue.

Count the number of cats you colored and underline that number.

Write your name at the top of the paper.

11

Follow the Directions:

Cross out five trees and four bears.

Count the number of things you crossed out and circle that number.

Write your name in orange at the bottom of the paper.

12

Follow the Directions:

Color three fish yellow and three fish orange.

Cut out five fish and paste them onto blue paper.

Write your name on the blue paper.

13

Follow the Directions:

Color four squares green and two circles red.

Count the number of things you colored and underline that number.

Write your name at the top of the paper.

14

Follow the Directions:

Cross out three birds, two trees, and one rabbit.

Count the number of things you crossed out and circle that number.

Write your name in red at the bottom of the paper.

15

Follow the Directions:

Color three birds orange.

Color two circles yellow.

Count the number of things you colored and underline that number.

Write your name at the bottom of the paper.

16

Follow the Directions:

Cross out three fish, four trees, and two flowers.

Count the number of things you crossed out and circle that number.

Write your name in blue at the top of the paper.

17

Follow the Directions:

Color three fish blue, five cats orange, and two squares red.

Count the number of things you colored and circle that number.

Write your name in green at the bottom of the paper.

18

Follow the Directions:

Cut out three circles and two squares.

Paste them onto white paper.

Color them blue.

Write your name on the paper.

Follow the Directions! Scholastic Professional Books

Section 6

19 Follow the Directions:

Cross out one fish, one rabbit, two birds, and two trees.

Count the number of things you crossed out and circle that number.

Write your name in green at the bottom of the paper.

20 Follow the Directions:

Underline one of each kind of animal.

Count the number of animals you underlined and underline that number.

Write your name in red at the top of the paper.

21 Follow the Directions:

Cross out three squares and three circles.

Underline one of the crossed-out squares.

Underline two of the crossed-out circles.

Write your name at the bottom of the paper.

22 Follow the Directions:

Cut out one tree, one flower, one square, and two circles.

Paste them onto orange paper.

Color the flower red.

Write your name on the orange paper.

23 Follow the Directions:

Underline two things that are not animals.

Color those two things blue.

Count the number of things you underlined and circle that number.

Write your name at the top of the paper.

24 Follow the Directions:

Circle one of each kind of animal.

Cross out the animal that lives in water.

Write your name in blue at the bottom of the paper.

Section 7

1

Follow the Directions:

Color three fish yellow.

Write your name at the top of the paper.

2

Follow the Directions:

Color two trees green.

Color three cats orange.

Write your name at the bottom of the paper.

3

Follow the Directions:

Color four birds blue.

Color one rabbit brown.

Count the number of things you colored and circle that number.

Write your name at the top of the paper.

4

Follow the Directions:

Cut out three trees and paste them onto green paper.

Write your name on the green paper.

5

Follow the Directions:

Cross out two circles and one flower.

Count the number of things you crossed out and circle that number.

Write your name at the top of the paper.

6

Follow the Directions:

Cut out two squares and two circles.

Paste them onto red paper.

Write your name on the red paper.

Follow the Directions! Scholastic Professional Books

7

Follow the Directions:

Color two bears brown, one cat orange, and one bird blue.

Write your name at the bottom of the paper.

8

Follow the Directions:

Circle the number three and color all the fish green.

Write your name at the top of the paper.

9

Follow the Directions:

Color all the flowers yellow.

Color all the circles orange.

Count the number of circles you colored.

Underline that number.

Write your name at the bottom of the paper.

10

Follow the Directions:

Circle the number five and color six squares blue.

Write your name at the top of the paper.

11

Follow the Directions:

Color all the rabbits brown.

Color all the flowers yellow.

Circle the number of flowers you colored.

Write your name at the bottom of the paper.

12

Follow the Directions:

Cross out the number three and color five bears blue.

Write your name at the top of the paper.

Section 7

13
Follow the Directions:

Color all the trees green.

Color all the bears blue.

Circle the number of trees you colored.

Write your name at the top of the paper.

14
Follow the Directions:

Cut out four rabbits and three flowers.

Paste them onto white paper and color them yellow.

Write your name on the paper.

15
Follow the Directions:

Circle the number one and color six cats yellow.

Write your name at the bottom of the paper.

16
Follow the Directions:

Color all the fish orange.

Color all the cats red.

Circle the number of cats you colored.

Write your name at the bottom of the paper.

17
Follow the Directions:

Cut out one fish and one bird.

Paste them onto white paper.

Color them blue.

Write your name on the paper.

18
Follow the Directions:

Circle the number four and color five birds red.

Write your name at the top of the paper.

Follow the Directions! Scholastic Professional Books

Section 7

19
Follow the Directions:

Cut out three bears.

Paste them onto white paper and color them brown.

Write your name on the paper.

20
Follow the Directions:

Color all the squares green.

Color all the circles orange.

Circle the number of squares you colored.

Write your name at the top of the paper.

21
Follow the Directions:

Cut out five squares and six circles.

Paste them onto white paper and color them all orange.

Write your name on the paper.

22
Follow the Directions:

Color five bears blue and circle the number three.

Write your name at the top of the paper.

23
Follow the Directions:

Circle the number two and color five squares orange.

Write your name at the bottom of the paper.

24
Follow the Directions:

Color four fish red and underline the number four.

Write your name at the top of the paper.

Section 8

1
Follow the Directions:

Count how many people in your class are wearing red today.

Write their names on a sheet of paper.

Write your name on the paper and leave it on your desk.

2
Follow the Directions:

Find something in the room that is shaped like a triangle.

Draw a picture of it.

Write your name on your paper.

Place it in the directions basket.

3
Follow the Directions:

Take out a sheet of paper.

Write the word *old* at the top of the paper.

Under that word, write three words that rhyme with *old*.

Write your name on the paper and put it in the directions basket.

4
Follow the Directions:

Find one thing in the room that is shaped like a rectangle.

On a sheet of paper, write a sentence about it.

Write your name on the paper and leave it on your desk.

Follow the Directions! Scholastic Professional Books

5

Follow the Directions:

What is your favorite book?

Write the title at the top of a sheet of paper.

Write two sentences about why you like that book.

Write your name on your paper and put it in the directions basket.

6

Follow the Directions:

Take out a sheet of paper.

Draw a circle on the paper.

Draw a triangle inside the circle.

Color the triangle blue.

Print your name below the circle.

Put your paper in the directions basket.

7

Follow the Directions:

On a sheet of paper, draw two big circles next to each other.

In one circle, write your name.

In the other circle, draw a picture of your favorite animal.

Leave your paper on your desk.

8

Follow the Directions:

Open a book to page 5.

Look for words that rhyme with *sat*.

Write the words on a sheet of paper.

Write your name on the back of the paper.

Put your paper in the directions basket.

9

Follow the Directions:

On a sheet of paper, write your name on the first line.

On the second line, write the first five letters of the alphabet.

On the third line, write a word that begins with *b*.

Put your paper in the directions basket.

10

Follow the Directions:

Take out a sheet of paper.

Write three sentences about something you saw on the way to school this morning.

Write your name on your paper and put it in the directions basket.

11

Follow the Directions:

Take out a sheet of paper.

Fold the paper in half.

On the inside, write your name and your age.

Leave your paper on your desk.

12

Follow the Directions:

Take out a sheet of paper.

Draw a triangle on the paper.

Write your name inside the triangle.

Put your paper in the directions basket.

Follow the Directions! Scholastic Professional Books

13

Follow the Directions:

On a sheet of paper, write your first and last name on the first line.

On the next line, write a sentence that tells one thing that you like to do after school.

Put your paper in the directions basket.

14

Follow the Directions:

Take out a sheet of paper.

Write the word *cat* on the first line.

Under that word, write four words that rhyme with *cat*.

Write your name at the bottom of the paper.

Put your paper in the directions basket.

15

Follow the Directions:

Find something in the room that is shaped like a square.

Draw a picture of it.

Write a sentence about it under the picture.

Write your name under the sentence.

Leave your paper on your desk.

16

Follow the Directions:

Count how many boys are wearing something blue.

Write the number on a sheet of paper.

Write your name on the back of the paper.

Put your paper in the directions basket.

17

Follow the Directions:

Count how many people in the room are wearing something red.

Write the number on a sheet of paper.

Write your name at the top of your paper.

Put your paper in the directions basket.

18

Follow the Directions:

Take out a sheet of paper.

Think of two words you like.

Use each word in a sentence.

Write your name below your sentences.

Put your paper in the directions basket.

19

Follow the Directions:

Take out a book or magazine.

Look for words that rhyme with *can*.

Write the words on a sheet of paper.

Write your name on the back of the paper.

Put your paper in the directions basket.

20

Follow the Directions:

On a sheet of paper, write three of your favorite foods.

Draw a picture of each one.

Write your name at the top of your paper.

Put your paper in the directions basket.

Follow the Directions! Scholastic Professional Books

1

Follow the Directions:

Lay your hand flat on a sheet of construction paper.

With a pencil, outline your hand on the paper.

Use your favorite color crayon to color the hand.

Cut out the outline of the hand.

Write your name on the back of the hand.

Put the hand in the directions basket.

2

Follow the Directions:

Take a sheet of paper from the directions basket.

Draw a big circle on the paper.

Draw a face inside the circle to show how you are feeling today.

Under the face, write a sentence that tells how you are feeling.

Write your name under the sentence.

Put your paper back in the directions basket.

3

Follow the Directions:

Take a sheet of paper from the directions basket.

On your paper, draw a picture of a friend.

Write three sentences about your friend.

Write your name under the sentences.

Tape your paper onto the board under the word *Friends*.

4

Follow the Directions:

Take a sheet of paper from the directions basket.

In the middle of your paper, draw a house.

On the right, draw three flowers.

On the left, draw a tree.

Color your picture.

Write your name at the top of the paper.

Put your paper back in the directions basket.

5

Follow the Directions:

Take an Activity Sheet from the directions basket.

Color the roof of the house blue.

Color the rest of the house yellow.

Color one flower red and one flower purple.

Color the cat pink.

Write your name at the top of the paper.

Put your paper in the directions basket.

6

Follow the Directions:

Take an Activity Sheet from the directions basket.

Color the tree green.

Color one flower pink, one flower purple, and one flower blue.

Cut out all the things you colored.

Paste the things onto another sheet of paper.

Write your name at the top of the paper.

Put your paper in the directions basket.

7

Follow the Directions:

Take an Activity Sheet from the directions basket.

Color the dog black.

Color the cat brown.

Color one flower red.

Color the tree green.

Cut out all the things you colored.

Paste them onto another sheet of paper.

Write your name on your finished project and put it in the directions basket.

8

Follow the Directions:

Take an Activity Sheet from the directions basket.

Color one flower pink and one flower blue.

Color the cat yellow.

Cut out the things you colored and paste them onto another sheet of paper.

Write your name on your finished project and put it in the directions basket.

Follow the Directions! Scholastic Professional Books

9

Follow the Directions:

Take an Activity Sheet from the directions basket.

Color the roof of the house one color.

Color the rest of the house another color.

Cut out the house and paste it onto another sheet of paper.

Write your name on your finished project and put it in the directions basket.

10

Follow the Directions:

Take a magazine or newspaper.

Find a picture of a car and cut it out.

Find a picture of a person and cut it out.

Find a picture of an animal and cut it out.

Paste the pictures onto a sheet of red paper.

Write your name on the paper and put it in the directions basket.

11

Follow the Directions:

Take a magazine or newspaper.

Find a picture of food and cut it out.

Find a picture of a child and cut it out.

Find a picture of a tree and cut it out.

Paste all your pictures onto a sheet of green paper.

Write your name on the paper and put it in the directions basket.

12

Follow the Directions:

Take a paper plate from the directions basket.

Look at the clown faces on the board.

Draw a clown face on your paper plate.

Write your name on the back of your plate.

Put your plate in the directions basket.

13

Follow the Directions:

Take a paper plate from the directions basket.

On the plate, draw two foods that you like.

On the plate, draw one food that you do not like.

Write your name on the back of the plate.

Put your plate in the directions basket.

14

Follow the Directions:

Take a sheet of paper from the directions basket.

Draw a picture of yourself on the paper.

Write your name under your picture.

Put your picture in the directions basket.

15

Follow the Directions:

Take a sheet of lined paper from the directions basket.

Write each letter of your name on a separate line.

Write a word that begins with each letter of your name. Try to think of words that describe you or things that you like.

Put your paper in the directions basket.

16

Follow the Directions:

Fold a sheet of paper in half.

Draw a birthday cake on the front.

Write *Happy Birthday* above the cake.

Draw _____ candles on the cake.

Write the birthday child's name under the cake.

Write a birthday message inside the card.

Put your card in the directions basket.

Follow the Directions! Scholastic Professional Books

Name:

Name:

Name:

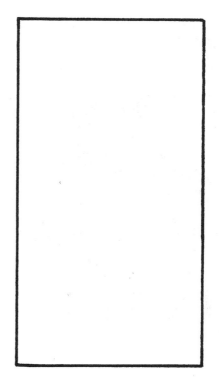

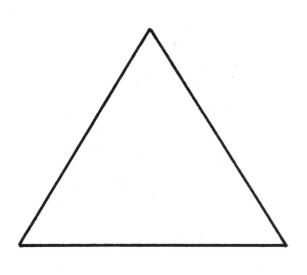

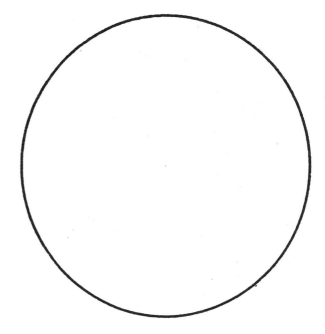

Name:

Follow the Directions! Scholastic Professional Books

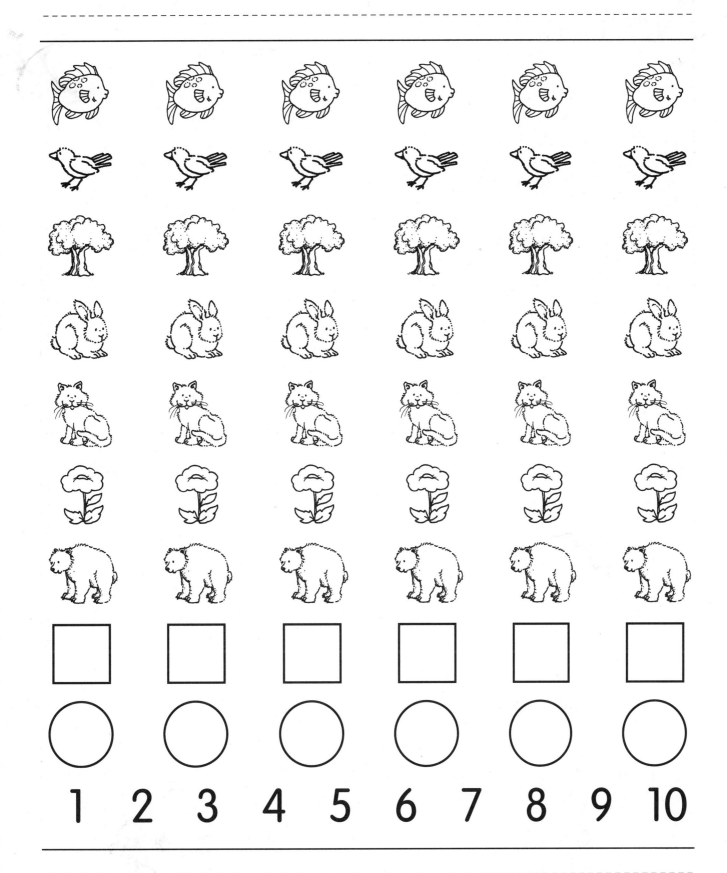

Name: ------------------------------

Follow the Directions! Scholastic Professional Books

Vocabulary Word List (Sections 1–5, 7)

a	fish	rabbit
all	five	rectangle
an	flower	red
and	follow	six
at	four	square
bear	green	sun
bird	house	that
black	inside	the
blue	it	them
book	line	things
bottom	name	three
brown	number	top
car	of	tree
cat	on	triangle
circle	onto	two
color	one	under
count	orange	underline
cross	out	white
cut	over	write
directions	paper	yellow
dog	paste	you
draw	purple	your

directions

underline

follow

circle

Follow the Directions! Scholastic Professional Books

red

green

color

blue

dog

house

yellow

flower

Follow the Directions! Scholastic Professional Books

it

write

car

the

name

black

your

brown

Follow the Directions! Scholastic Professional Books

orange

tree

purple

cat

sun

triangle

book

square

Follow the Directions! Scholastic Professional Books

cross

paste

rectangle

out

cut

under

onto

over

Follow the Directions! Scholastic Professional Books

draw

an

inside

a

top

bottom

on

of

Follow the Directions! Scholastic Professional Books

at

two

paper

one

four

six

three

five

Follow the Directions! Scholastic Professional Books

rabbit

bird

bear

fish

count

line

white

number

Follow the Directions! Scholastic Professional Books

you

that

things

and

all

them

Follow the Directions! Scholastic Professional Books